# ALEXANDER PUSHKIN

## *Epigrams*
## *&*
## *Satirical*
## *Verse*

### Edited and Translated by
### Cynthia Whittaker

Ardis, Ann Arbor

The illustrations in this book are pen-and-ink drawings by A. S. Pushkin

Ardis Publishers
2901 Heatherway
Ann Arbor, Michigan 48104

Library of Congress Cataloging in Publication Data

Pushkin, Aleksandr Sergeevich, 1799-1837.
    Alexander Pushkin, epigrams and satirical verse.

    Bibliography: p.
    1. Pushkin, Aleksandr Sergeevich, 1799-1837—
Translations, English.    I. Whittaker, Cynthia H., 1941-
II. Title.
PG3347.A17   1984    891.71'3        84-253
ISBN 0-88233-886-2
ISBN 0-88233-887-0 (pbk.)

*To my parents,*
*    Jean and Leon Hyla, and*
*To my second mother,*
*    Maria Tolstoy*

*A Devil Warming His Feet by the Fire*
Kishinev, 1821

# CONTENTS

Acknowledgments  xiii

Introduction  1

## I: EPIGRAMS ON EPIGRAMS

1. "Oh muse of fire-breathing satire!"  11
2. The Prose Writer and the Poet  12
3. Advice  13
4. To My Friends  13
5. Ex Ungue Leonem  14

## II. POLITICAL FIGURES AND THEMES

6. "There's one grande dame I've pity for"  17
7. You and I  19
8. Inscription on the Gates at Ekaterinhof  21
9. "We will amuse good citizens a little"  22
10. On Karamzin  23
11. Fairy Tales (Noël)  24
12. On Alexander I  26
13. To Two Men Named Alexander Pavlovich  27
14. To the Bust of a Conqueror  28
15. "He spent his whole life on the road"  29
16. On Arakcheev: "Of all Russia, oppressor"  30
17. On Arakcheev: "He's a corporal in the capital"  31
18. On Sturdza: "A soldier crowned you serve as lackey"  32
19. On Sturdza: "I walk around Sturdza"  33
20. "The Bible men enjoy such bliss"  34
21. On Count A. K. Razumovsky  35
22. On Prince A. N. Golitsyn  36

23. "Oh Princes, eminent patricians"   *37*

24. " 'Though not midst us, but where I can't record"   *38*

25. On Vorontsov: "Half milord, and half a
    tradesman"   *39*

26. On Vorontsov: "The singer David, small of
    stature"   *39*

27. To a Portrait of Chaadaev   *40*

28. Epigram (From an Anthology)   *41*

29. To Andrew Muravyov   *42*

30. To Kankrin   *43*

31. "It's feign to trust a gambler's honor"   *44*

32. "When the Academy meets"   *45*

## III. LITERARY FIGURES AND THEMES

33. The Story of a Versifier   *49*

34. On Rybushkin   *50*

35. "A sullen troika now sings off"   *51*

36. Epigram: " 'Ristophanes did promise us the kind of tragic
    drama"   *52*

37. On Puchkova: "Puchkova we really shouldn't
    gibe"   *53*

38. On Puchkova: "Oh why cry out that you're a
    *virgin*"   *53*

39. On Th. N. Glinka   *54*

40. Epigram (On Karamzin)   *55*

41. "Oh grandpa, listen, everytime it seems"   *56*

42. "Here's Willy—he's so full of love's fire"   *57*

43. Epigram on the Death of a Poet   *57*

44. "At supper I did eat o'er much"   *58*

45. The Misfortune of Klit   *59*

46. On the Translation of *The Iliad*   *60*

47. On the Tragedy of Count Khvostov   *61*

48. "Although sympathy won't help"   *62*

49. Epigram: "Oh hoary Hisser, you have reigned with
    glory"   *63*

50. Epigram: "A hymn was offered Phoebus by an urchin"  64
51. The Nightingale and the Cuckoo  65
52. An Epigram on Shalikov  66
53. "How awful for our native land—Lishchinsky's done in!"  67
54. A Good Fellow  67
55. "Oh, please, Fedorov, don't come to visit me"  68

## IV. JOURNALISTS AND JOURNALISM

56. A Collection of Insects  71
57. "If foolishly you'd start a-writing"  72
58. "Timkovsky ruled supreme—and all aloud did say"  73
59. "In vain was Europe gasping"  74
60. To N. N.  75
61. On Kachenovsky: "Oh critic crushed by an immortal hand"  76
62. "*Messenger of Europe* and *Son of the Fatherland*"  77
63. On Kachenovsky: "Swineopoulous! Incorrigibly flinging curses"  78
64. "Although he's fairly good as poet"  79
65. "How is it you're not bored with scolding?"  79
66. On Kachenovsky: "Untalented in his slandering"  80
67. "He hunts out journalistic feuding"  80
68. "Attacked by female indisposition"  81
69. There's Life in the Old Dog Yet!  82
70. The Literary News  83
71. "When I muddied the face of the critic"  84
72. Epigram: "The journals had offended him so cruelly"  85
73. On Nadezhdin  86
74. "Into a journal, no wit European"  87
75. The Cobbler (A Parable)  88
76. On Bulgarin  89
77. Epigram: "It's not so bad, Advei Fliugarin"  90

78. "That you're a Pole is no taboo"  90
79. "When I shall find Madame Potemkin"  91
80. "If you walk into Smirdin's"  92

## V. INDIVIDUALS

81. A Portrait  95
82. "Hauenschild and Engelhardt"  96
83. An Inquisitive Person  97
84. "You've had luck with ninnies charming"  98
85. "Oh Beverly-Horace, poet-gambler"  99
86. Epigram (On Count F. I. Tolstoi)  100
87. 'Your guesses—they are all in vain"  101
88. "Departed author, spare and puny"  101
89. On A. F. Orlov  102
90. On the Marriage of General N. M. Sipiagin  103
91. On K. Dembrovsky  104
92. A Complaint  105
93. On Lanov  106
94. "Prince G.'s a type unknown to me"  107
95. "If you forsake the pharmacy for some laurel
      wreathing"  108
96. "Punish him, oh saints above"  109
97. To Ogareva  110
98. On Photius  111
99. To Countess Orlova-Chesmenskaya  112
100. A Conversation Between Photius and Countess
      Orlova  112
101. The Bishop  113
102. Christ Has Risen  114
103. On Kolosova  115
104. To Nimfodora Semenova  116
105. "Has Clarise but little money"  117
106. "Lisa's scared to fall in love"  117
107. "Tadarashka loves you sure"  118
108. Madrigal  119

109. Epigram: "While leaving honor to a fate so feckless"    *120*

110. On A. A. Davydova    *121*

111. Epigram: "So captivated am I by your matron"    *122*

112. Epigram: "Get treatment—Pangloss' fate will you appoint"    *123*

A Bibliographical Note    *125*

# ACKNOWLEDGMENTS

Two scholars assisted me greatly in the composition of this book. Professor Maurice Friedberg of the University of Illinois, so well-known among Slavicists both for his ability as a literary critic and for his marvelous wit, warmly encouraged the unveiling of Pushkin's humor to an English-reading audience. He also generously read through the translations and provided keen observations about the epigrams' many innuendos. Professor Maria Tolstoy, emeritus of Hunter College, with her perfect knowledge of both English and Russian, spent days with me making sure that the translations duplicated Pushkin's exact, precise meaning. I am also grateful to the Released Time Program of the School of Liberal Arts & Sciences at Baruch College for granting three semesters of a reduced teaching schedule in order to allow the extra time needed for completion of the manuscript.

# ALEXANDER PUSHKIN

## *Epigrams*
## *&*
## *Satirical*
## *Verse*

# INTRODUCTION

Alexander Pushkin, who lived from 1799 to 1837, during his short life gained a place as Russia's greatest poet and as one of the immortals in world literature. It is not so well known, however, that Pushkin ranks just as high as an epigrammatist. The poet's epigrams were not published as a separate volume in Russian until 1979,[1] and very few have been translated into any language. Several reasons may account for this neglect. To begin with, the epigrams appear untranslatable since they are usually structured around the use of a pun. In addition, epigrams, by their very nature, never deal with universal themes but relate specifically to a single episode or person; consequently, unless the circumstances are explained, the point of an epigram may be lost days, let alone years, after its composition. Furthermore, while Pushkin's epigrams are often alluded to in studies of the poet as supporting evidence for some one of his opinions, the epigrams themselves are not taken very seriously, probably because they are humorous, and are dismissed as light verse. This inattention, though, has represented a major loss to nineteenth-century Russian cultural history.

Pushkin himself took his epigrams quite seriously. He regarded them as his best weapons for felling opponents, critics, or whomever and whatever he found distasteful. The use of this type of verse was to him much like participating in a pistol duel, where all depends on one well-placed shot—and it comes as no surprise that Pushkin died of wounds inflicted in just such a duel. The poet recognized the epigrammatic *genre* as a demanding art form. Employing brevity, polish, pithiness, a tense and logical construction, building only upon a few lines of verse and relying upon the power of rhyme and meter, the epigram must swiftly and cleverly rush to the last line where it demolishes the object of satire or caricature. The writer of good epigrams thus requires a rare combination of poetic talent, linguistic precision, deep convictions, mordant wit, spleen and love of combat; Pushkin possessed all these traits in abundance.

1

In general terms, epigrams constitute unique tools for studying a culture, particularly one where the press is censored. Such verses are normally not published during the author's own era because they blaspheme the sacred bases of the status quo: heads of government, their ministers, the clergy, or certain institutions, such as the censorship itself. In other cases, epigrams sometimes use scatological language or so clearly attack the honor of individuals that, whether or not charges such as immorality or greed are warranted, normal codes of civilized behavior prevent their reaching print.

In this manner, epigrams become a form of elite folklore; the verses are relayed by word of mouth at salons or other social gatherings where the literate upper classes meet. Once an epigram achieves widespread popularity, the historian can, I think, assume that the audience is not only entertained but recognizes a ring of truth, or even gives approval, which the authorities find threatening. For instance, Pushkin's caricature of Tsar Alexander I (1801-25) in "Noel" as a self-serving hypocrite was the first step leading to the poet's banishment from St. Petersburg in 1820; Governor-General Michael Vorontsov evicted Pushkin from Odessa in 1824 once epigrams circulated in the city which labeled this leading official as a self-important, posturing opportunist who lacked qualities of nobility. In essence, epigrams provide insights into the unofficial climate of opinion.

Although epigrams belong to every epoch, in modern Europe, they appear to enjoy their golden ages in eras of transition, for example in early seventeenth-century England (Donne, Jonson), in eighteenth-century German society (Lessing, Herder, Goethe), in the French Enlightenment (Boileau, Voltaire), or in what is often called pre-reform Russia, the reigns of Alexander and of Nicholas I (1825-55). Since these are historical periods when change is imminent but not yet forthcoming, critical thought, plans for reform, divisions of opinion and conflicting parties proliferate, whether on political, social or literary questions. Since the object of an epigrammatist is to take an adversarial position on some issue or person, such an atmosphere is conducive to his emergence. In addition, the

2

humor, wit, scorn or malice that epigrams display offer psychological outlets for impatience, ire or even simple disgust with incompetence, pretense or arrogance.

The Soviet literary scholar, L. F. Ershov, suggests that the epigram provides a "miniature" of the clashes of its era, although he overstates his case when he begins to elaborate on this basically valid opinion.[2] By the time Pushkin reached adolescence, Russia, too, was experiencing that traumatic period of growth. In the eighteenth century, the country had become a regular member of the European family of nations but was still regarded as a younger brother. In 1812, the Russians dealt Napoleon his first serious defeat, and Tsar Alexander marched at the head of the allied armies that finally unseated the French Emperor. These events resulted in a blossoming of national pride as well as in an era of self-searching among Russian intellectuals. They faced the seemingly eternal "accursed" or "burning" questions of what their nation's relationship should be to the West, how and what Russia could contribute to world culture and by what means it should develop politically and socially. Since no one quite knew, a variety of answers arose, and this lent an ebullient, if somewhat chaotic, atmosphere to the era.

In the early nineteenth century, Russian men of letters were painfully aware that they possessed only a fledgling culture. Indeed, the first analysis of the Russian literary language was made only in the mid-eighteenth century by Michael Lomonosov, a brilliant scholar in a variety of fields including linguistics. He concluded that Russian literature demanded a "high"—and soon to be called "old"—style which preserved the character of the non-vernacular, medieval Church Slavonic that formed the historic roots of the language. Much of the literature that followed this theory appeared archaic, cumbersome and bombastic since it bore little resemblance to spoken Russian. Nonetheless, the Old Style enjoyed a significant following among men of letters, who equated it with true national tradition and saw in it a relection of national character; they also bore a fear, which often became xenophobic, that contact with Western literary forms and linguistic styles would result in an

3

imitative and sterile Russian culture.

At the turn of the century, Nicholas Karamzin, then Russia's most important belletrist, advocated a "new" literary language that was more simple, lively, graceful and colloquial and that jettisoned Church Slavonic vocabulary in favor of gallicisms or new Russian words that expressed modern ideas and emotions. Karamzin also supported the introduction of new Western forms, such as the ballad and short story. His ideas enjoyed a significant following, especially among younger Russian men of letters, who went on to experiment with sentimentalism, neoclassicism and romanticism and who believed that contact with foreign trends could only enrich Russian culture. This approach to literature triumphed.[3]

Despite the continuing activity of a few supporters of the Old Style, the adherents of the New Style, in 1815, in celebration, formed the Arzamas literary circle. Pushkin joined it upon his graduation from Tsarskoe Selo Lycée in 1817. The group fell apart a year later but not before its members passed on to the young poet their esteem for classical form, modern expression, catholic taste and Russian themes that Pushkin's genius combined and that provided the foundation for the nation's golden ages of poetry and prose.[4] Hence, Pushkin would direct many epigrams against the remaining defenders of the Old Style.

Political and social questions also engendered heated debates in the first decades of the nineteenth century in Russia. Soviet scholars, to the point of utter boredom, insist on seeing in Pushkin a precursor of Lenin.[5] Although S. L. Frank's view of the poet as a "liberal conservative" is more convincing, he also exaggerated when he claimed that Pushkin was "the greatest Russian political thinker in the nineteenth century."[6] The epigrams on Alexander I, which depict the monarch as a hypocrite, are in fact "miniatures" of the general feelings among progressive members of Russia's intelligentsia: he championed constitutional monarchies while abroad but retained despotism at home; he advocated projects for freeing serfs but retained the inhumane institution; he brought Russia military renown in the Napoleonic campaigns but lost his position of leadership in

4

foreign policy after 1815; he took an ecumenical view toward religion but then returned to proselytizing the stiff formalism of Orthodoxy; he established the first ministry of education in Russia but let it fall under the reign of obscurantists. Hope mixed with despair and led to the fiasco of the Decembrist Revolt in 1825 that was triggered by Alexander's death and the accession of Nicholas I.

Until about 1840, that is, until the time of Pushkin's death, Nicholas held out hope that he would reform his realm gradually, and the poet held his pen. Although the Tsar and Pushkin had a complicated relationship, Pushkin respected him as a monarch more than Alexander.[7] In all, Pushkin, like the majority of his older brothers in Arzamas, was keenly disappointed that Alexander had not carried out his promises of political and social reform. On the other hand, these men could not accept revolutionary means to achieve these ends and were aghast at the Decembrist Revolt.

In the next reign, they continued to hope for reform from above, which was, after all, the Russian national tradition, the link to historical continuity and the alternative to violent upheaval. They also assumed that the nobility, the natural cultural and political elite, would help devise plans for their country's progress. Pushkin, in addition, was a Great Russian nationalist who could not tolerate, for instance, the revolt of the Poles against Russian stewardship in 1830 31.[8] Thus, the ardent lover of freedom in his youth, as shown in his epigrams and other "liberal" verses, decried revolutionary means when they were attempted and placed his hopes, in accordance with Russian tradition, in the hands of an enlightened tsar assisted by a cultured nobility.[9] After 1825, Pushkin's epigrams are much less political and deal almost entirely with those who fail to revere his literary genius and with those members of the nobility whom he found unworthy of their high calling in society.

Pushkin's "miniatures," since they provide evidence of the concerns of his era, are divided thematically in this volume. A chronological division possesses only the advantage of demonstrating the clumsiness and artlessness of the ten epigrams written before 1817, when Pushkin was in his early teens.

Except for four later epigrams, the remainder were written between 1817 and 1830 and are more easily understood, more logical and offer a clearer view of the cultural era when organized according to subject matter. The choice of epigrams was based on two criteria: those that offered the best sampling of the art or those that the poet himself labeled epigrams. Thus, some rather fine examples of satirical verse are not included, for instance "On the Recovery of Lucullus," since they are too long to qualify as epigrams; epigrammatic passages in Pushkin's longer works, such as *Eugene Onegin* or "Letter to a Censor," are also omitted because they were not intended specifically as epigrams.

In the epigrams in Part I, Pushkin simply renders homage to his appreciation of the *genre* as the best weapon with which to insult one's literary opponents. Part II provides a vivid picture of the poet's hostility to absolutism, incompetent monarchs and officials who were either oppressive, stupid, foolish, immoral, fawning, or, in general, brought Russia dishonor. In Part III, Pushkin is the most playful; he pokes fun at litterateurs who possess aspirations or a self-importance incommensurate with their talent. When he turns to journalists, Pushkin is much more vicious since these are the people who neglect to recognize his great talent and genius, something of which he was pridefully and compulsively aware. While Pushkin himself was noted for his difficult personality—he could be nasty, irascible, vain, haughty, unkind, greedy, promiscuous, given to gambling and drink, irresponsible, self-righteous, self-centered, puerile[10]—he picked out for attack, sometimes with malice and sometimes with good humor, his acquaintances who possessed many of these same qualities.

Vasily Zhukovsky, another great poet but also a heralded translator of poetry in Pushkin's era, made the well-known comment that "a translator of prose is a slave—a translator of poetry is a competitor." Nonetheless, since I am not a Zhukovsky, in this translation I remain more a slave. Because the power of an epigram depends so heavily on meter and rhyme, I felt compelled to imitate that of Pushkin as closely as possible and did not even contemplate the kind of artistic freedom that might render the poet in blank verse. In fact, when I occasionally thought Pushkin lacking (some of his epigrams were, after all, childish or extemporaneous), I did not try to adjust his words or form. What I especially tried to do was to reproduce in English Pushkin's use of *double entendres*, the pun, the repetition of similar words, root words and vowels, and the use of onomatopoeia and alliteration in the epigrams. Ironically enough, the most difficult problem in translation was to replicate Pushkin's simplicity of speech; despite all his vituperation, he only occasionally used slang expressions or "attack words." This translation, I should add, contains no words or phrases that were not in use in English in Pushkin's era. Such challenges are not without their rewards; the hours spent with Pushkin were a thorough joy.

Cynthia H. Whittaker
Baruch College of the City University of New York

April 1983

# NOTES

1. A. S. Pushkin, *Epigrammy* (Moscow, 1979). Even only a few articles deal with this aspect of Pushkin's work separately: G. Glebov, "Filosofskaia epigramma Pushkina," *Vremennik pushkinskoi komissii*, III (1937), 399-400; I. Kazantsev, "Iazyk i stil' pushkinskikh epigramm," *Uchenye zapiski*, VI (Perm, 1940), 49-108; N. Lerner, "Pushkin, Fotii i gr. Orlova," *Golos minuvshego*, IV (April 1913), 82-84; P. O. Morozov, "Epigramma Pushkina na perevod Iliady," *Pushkin i ego sovremenniki*, IV, 13 (1913), 13-17.

2. Two Soviet studies deal with the Russian epigram in forewords to books containing wide selections of examples of the *genre*: V. Manuilov, "Predislovie," *Russkaia epigramma (XVIII-XIX vv.)* (Leningrad, 1958), 5-28; L. F. Ershov, "O russkoi epigramme," *Russkaia epigramma vtoroi poloviny XVII-nachala XXv.* (Leningrad, 1975), 5-56. The latter volume also contains excellent scholarly notes on pp. 617-909.

3. "Shishkovisty i karamzinisty," in V. Orlov, ed., *Epigramma i satira: Iz istorii literaturnoi borby XIX-go veka, I (1800-1840)* (Moscow, 1931), 3-132; I. Tynianov, *Arkhaisty i novatory* (Leningrad, 1929).

4. P. V. Annenkov, A. S. *Pushkin v aleksandrovskuiu epokhu, 1799-1826 gg.* (St. Petersburg, 1874), 57-125, 293-332; D. D. Blagoi, *Tvorcheskii put' Pushkina (1813-1826)* (Moscow, 1950), 182-85; N. L. Brodskii, ed., *Pushkin v shkole* (Moscow, 1951), especially pp. 307-17; M. I. Gillel'son, *Molodoi Pushkin i arzamasskoe bratstvo* (Leningrad, 1974); K. I. Grot, *Pushkinskii litsei* (St. Petersburg, 1911); B. Meilakh, *Pushkin i ego epokha* (Moscow, 1958), 260-82.

5. See, for example: B. P. Gorodetskii, ed., *Pushkin: Itogi i problemy izucheniia* (Moscow, 1966).

6. S. L. Frank, *Pushkin kak politicheskii myslitel'* (Belgrade, 1937), 42 pp. The quote is on p. 14; the volume also contains an illuminating introduction and afterword by Peter Struve. Also see L. Schapiro, *Rationalism and Nationalism in Russian Nineteenth-Century Political Thought* (New Haven, 1967), 45-58.

7. G. Schramm, "Ein Dichter und ein Kaiser: Pushkin und Nikoiaus I," *Festschrift fur Fritz T. Epstein zum 80. Geburtstag* (Wiesbaden, 1978), 42-55.

8. P. E. Shchegolev, *Iz zhizni i tvorchestva Pushkina* (Moscow, 1931), 351-54.

9. On this epoch in Pushkin's life, consult: A. S. Pushkin: *Dnevnik A. S. Pushkina, 1833-1835* (Moscow, 1923), 66-67 and "Zametki o russkom dvorian-stve," *Pol'noe sobranie sochinenii*, VI, 352-54; I. L. Feinberg, *Nezavershennye raboty Pushkina* (Moscow, 1958), 278-91; N. Lerner, "Pushkin v Moskve posle ssylki," *Biblioteka velikikh pisatelei: Pushkin*, III (Petrograd, 1915), 335-52; A. Tseitlin, "Zapiski Pushkina o narodnom vospitanii," *Literaturnyi sovremennik*, 1 (Jan 1937), 266-91; V. Vodovozov, "Politicheskie i obshchestvennye vzgliady Pushkina v poslednii period ego zhizni," *Biblioteka*, VI, 368-89.

10. For books that emphasize Pushkin's picaresque traits, consult: P. K. Guber, *Don-Zhuanskii spisok* (Petrograd, 1923); M. L. Hofmann, *Pushkin Don-Juan* (Paris, 1935); V. Veresaev, *Pushkin v zhizni*, 2 vols. (Moscow, 1936).

# I

# EPIGRAMS ON EPIGRAMS

И Флористского неона.
Съ нимъ тайный убиецъ разделяетъ,
На нихъ потоатъ игривый вздоръ,
Съ небесной грацiю сливаетъ
Очей и знаковъ разговоръ;
Поетъ ему и пѣсни горъ,
И пѣсни Грузiи шутливой
И памяти нетерпѣливой
Передаетъ языкъ чужой

Впервые Литвинской душой
Она любила, знала шалить,
Но Русской души молодой
Давно утратитъ простоту.
Не мочь она сердцемъ отвѣчатъ
любви младенской, открытой
И можетъ бытъ, [  ] забытый
Тоскъ она воспоминаетъ

Не вдругъ увянетъ наша младость
Не вдругъ восторги бросятъ насъ
И неожиданную радость
Еще обнимемъ мы не разъ

2.

Self-Portrait, Head of a Youth
Kishinev, 1822

From 1824 to 1826, Pushkin lived in enforced and lonely exile on his mother's estate in Mikhailovskoe, near Pskov. Although this isolation resulted in one of the most productive periods in his artistic life, the poet chafed at being cut off from social and cultural contacts and resented his surveillance by local religious and civil authorities. His desire that the Tsar grant him a pardon meant keeping out of trouble and silencing his acerbic comments or at least publishing them anonymously. In the privacy of his cluttered study, though, Pushkin prepared to publish a collection of epigrams; he never completed the project but during his exile composed the following five introductory pieces. Calling upon the inspiration of Juvenal, the first-century Latin satirical poet, Pushkin relished the notion of felling his literary and political enemies by means of epigrammatic quick wit.

---

I.

Oh muse of fire-breathing satire!
Please come unto my beck'ning call!
I do not need a thundrous lyre,
Just pass the whip of Juvenal!
For neither imitators gelid,
Nor those who translate empty-bellied,
Nor rhymers meek and unaware,
My plaguing epigrams do I prepare!
Peace unto you, you luckless rhymesters,
Peace unto you, you journal staffers,
Peace unto you, you humble fools!
But you, who form a scoundrels' school—
To arms! Of all you dregs I'll be tormentor,
Your punishment will be of shame!
But, sirs, do give me a reminder,
If someone I forget to name!
How many milksops are there shameless,

11

How many blockheads widely famous,
Are ready now to get from me
A brand for all eternity!

(1824-25)


## 2. THE PROSE WRITER AND THE POET


O'er what, prose writer, are you fussing?
Just give me any thought you're mulling:
I'll make its end a sharpened tip,
With flying rhyme I'll feather it,
I'll place it on a tight-drawn bowstring,
Into an arc I'll bend the pliant bow,
With venture, I will do the aiming,
And woe will come unto our foe!

(1825)

## 3. ADVICE

Pay heed: Whenever journalistic swarms
Of gnats and horseflies round you are aflying,
Don't argue, bother not with courteous forms,
And don't protest their squeaks or brazen crying:
Dear friend, with neither logic nor with taste
Can ever one subdue this ilk so stubborn.
It's sinful to get angry; just take your aim and then posthaste
Slam down a nimble epigram to stun them.

(1825)

## 4. TO MY FRIENDS

My enemies, for now I am quite silent . . .
And, seemingly, my temper quick has lost its fight,
But none of you do I let out of sight,
And someday I'll pick one of you as target:
My penetrating claws he'll not outpace
Since I'll attack with speed and without mercy.
I'll circle skies much like the hawk who's greedy
And keeps a watch for turkeys and for geese.

(1825)

"To My Friends" received a polemical response from Alexander Izmailov (1779-1831), a writer of fables and publisher of the journal *The Loyalist*. Pushkin, who prided himself on never turning down a challenge, responded with the following epigram which referred to Izmailov's "asses' ears," the symbol in myths and fables of an ignoramus. Also, Pushkin sported enormously long fingernails, his "claws," as he called them.

---

## 5. *EX UNGUE LEONEM*

Not long ago, I whistled off some verse
And let its publication go without my name;
One journal's wagwit pried some small response;
Without his name, he let it into print, the man of shame.
So what? Not I, nor let alone that vulgar wagwit,
Successfully could hide our little pranks:
He by my claws did know me in a minute,
I by his ears did know him in a shake.

(1825)

# II

# POLITICAL FIGURES AND THEMES

Portrait of Voltaire, Self-Portrait, Profiles
Mikhailovskoe, 1824

This verse satirized the ambivalent nature of the reign of Catherine II (1762-96). Her reputation, which brought her the epithet "the Great," rested on her expansive foreign policy. The satire, for instance, recalls the taking of the Prague fortress in Warsaw, the defeat of the Turks, the burning of Turkish and Swedish fleets and the annexation of the Crimea.

Catherine also won applause for her "progressive" domestic policy, much of which, however, was window dressing. She did indeed promote learning and herself wrote plays and articles and dabbled in scholarship. She courted intellectuals throughout Europe, and they pronounced her an enlightened monarch for promulgating instructions to a Russian legislative commission based on the ideas of Montesquieu and Beccaria. Few noted that nothing practical emerged from her plans or her association with *philosophes* such as Voltaire. Catherine also gained notoriety for her numerous liaisons; this led to sordid speculation about the circumstances of her death. In all, though, Pushkin seemed nostalgic for the era when Russia was considered a serious center of European culture.

Gabriel Derzhavin (1743-1816) was a leading eighteenth-century poet. Count Gregory Orlov (1734-83) helped Catherine seize the throne from her husband and was one of her longtime favorites and lovers. Prince Karl Joseph de Ligne (1735-1814), a master of the *bon mot*, was an Austrian diplomat, prolific author and good friend of the Empress. Ivan Barkov (1732-68) wrote popular pornographic poetry.

---

6.

There's one grande dame I've pity for,
A woman who was surely anxious
For glories varied: smoke of war
And smoke of incense from Parnassus.
The fortress /Prague/ we owe to her,
Enlightenment and the Crimea;
Of the Crescent, humiliator,
We ought now to name her
Our muse, Melpómene, Minerva.
On Tsárskoe Sélo's treed walks,
She with Derzhávin and Orlóv
Did carry on some learned talks—

/She had tea—/
With de Ligne—and sometimes with Barkóv.
This sweet old lady lived out her days
Agreeably and somewhat like a harlot;
She of Voltaire best friend became,
She wrote an edict, fleets she flamed,
And died while sitting on the toilet.
/From then/, a haze.
Oh, Russia, hapless realm,
Your glory, choked, dishelmed,
With Catherine was razed.

(1824)

Pushkin, beginning in his teens, often expressed progressive political attitudes and especially a bitterness toward the autocracy. These tendencies were encouraged by his new friends in the Arzamas literary circle, which he joined just after his graduation from Tsarskoe Selo Lycée in 1817, but the group disbanded one year later. A few of its members became Decembrists, although the majority simply felt keen disappointment that Tsar Alexander I (1801-25) was retreating from the progressive domestic and foreign policies he had seemed to espouse earlier in his reign. In addition, the poet, who struggled with financial problems all his adult life, could resent anyone living in easy luxury—hence "You and I."

Count Dmitry Khvostov (1756-1835), a prolific poet and dramatist, was a favorite target of Arzamas members because he adhered to the eighteenth-century Russian style of writing, which the younger litterateurs rightfully deemed turgid and bombastic. Old newsprint, by the way, was often used as toilet paper.

---

## 7. YOU AND I

I'm so poor, while you're a rich man;
I'm a poet, you pen prose instead;
You're complexioned poppy-red;
I, like death, am gaunt and ashen.
Having never any cares,
You live in a mammoth dwelling;
I amid my woes and snares
Spend my days on straw a-lying.
Everyday you eat foods fancy,
You sip wines when e'er you feature,
And not rarely you're too lazy
To respond to calls of nature.
I must do with stale shards;
Drinking water that's unhealthy,
From my loft, two hundred yards
Must I dash when nature calls me.
Circled by a crowd of slaves,

With a despot's glance so fearsome,
Your own arse so plump and suave
You do wipe with cloths of cotton;
My own asshole, plain of type,
Cradling care is no resource;
With Khvostóv's one ode so coarse,
Though I'm wincing, do I wipe.

(1817-20)

In 1824, Khvostov wrote a poem, "A May Walk in Ekaterinhof" and dedicated it to Count Michael Miloradovich (1771-1825), the military governor of St. Petersburg. In 1820, the Tsar had ordered Miloradovich's agents to search Pushkin's quarters for "disloyal" poetry, and then the general interrogated him. However, contemporaries attested that Miloradovich convinced Alexander to ease Pushkin's sentence from exile in Siberia to government service in the pleasant clime of southern Russia.

Pushkin, like most of his countrymen, considered Peter, whose reign extended from 1682 to 1725, the founder of the modern autocratic state in Russia. Ekaterinhof was a palace and park built on the Neva River by Peter the Great and sometimes used by Miloradovich for revelling.

---

## 8. INSCRIPTION ON THE GATES AT EKATERINHOF

This hole 'bout which one time before Khvostóv
        did sing!
Proclaim do you the Russian landscape's stinginess,
 Peter the autocratic king
 And Milorádovich's foolishness.

(1826-30)

This epigram is based on a French revolutionary couplet. A textbook in use at Pushkin's Lycée, *A Course in Ancient and Modern Literature*, related the verse but lamented that some people found it amusing.

---

9.

We will amuse good citizens a little
And at the pillory where one's disgraced,
We'll use the guts of the last of the priests
The last of the tsars to strangle.

(1817-19)

Nicholas Karamzin (1766-1826), having already established himself as one of his country's leading and most innovative prose writers, in 1803 decided to turn his talents to the fledgling field of Russian history. He envisioned a magisterial work that would cover the origins of the state in the ninth century to modern times. As the volumes of Karamzin's *History of the Russian State* began to appear, Pushkin noted and objected to the thesis that Russia was and would remain a mighty country only with the preservation of the institution of autocracy, the Russian form of despotism.

---

## 10. ON KARAMZIN

In his *History*, there is elegance, simplicity
That prove to us without the slightest prejudice or doubt
    That the autocracy is a necessity
      And delightful is the knout.

(1818)

"Christmans Fairy Tales" imitated the French tradition of "noels," or yuletide satires. The epigram is replete with references to contemporary events and personalities. Tsar Alexander I was known as the "Savior of Europe" and was highly touted in the Western press for his leading role in defeating Napoleon in 1814-15. Alexander actively participated in the subsequent congresses of the newly formed Concert of Europe. On December 22, 1818, he had just returned from the one held in Aachen; during his peregrinations, the Tsar had paraded in the uniforms of his Austrian and Prussian allies. Earlier that year, the Tsar addressed a meeting of the Polish Sejm (Parliament) and implied that he would introduce a constitution and civil rights in Russia, but only when the country had reached "maturity." Alexander did not convince Pushkin he would carry out his promises. Ivan Lavrov, Vasily Sots and Ivan Gorgoli were, respectively, executive director of the police, theater censor, and chief of the St. Petersburg police, all of whom had had run-ins with Pushkin. The satire became famous overnight and figured as one reason for the poet's banishment from the capital in 1820.

---

## 11. FAIRY TALES

### Noel

Hurrah! To Russia gallops
The despot who has roamed.
The Christ shed bitter teardrops
And, withal, people moaned.
Now, Mary, troubled, scares the Savior with a saying:
   "Oh, Baby, cry not, cry not, Sire:
   Bogeyman'll get you—the Russian tsar!"
    The Tsar walks in, pontificating:

     "The rest of the world is informed,
     But learn, oh people Russian:
     I made myself two uniforms,
     Both Austrian and Prussian.

Rejoice, oh nation mine; I'm fit and stout and sated:
 My name the newsmen glorified;
 I ate and drank and certified—
  And work on me ne'er grated.

 And listen, in addition,
 To then what I'll espouse:
 Lavróv will get a pension
 And Sots the crazy house;
With the rule of law, Gorgóli I'll replace,
 And to people, people's rights,
 By dint of royal will and might,
  I'll bestow with grace."

 In bed, from jubilation,
 The Babe burst into tears:
 "Is this not joculation?
 Is all this really near?"
Then mother said to Him: "Close your eyes, don't wail;
 It's time to go to sleep, by far,
 But listen how our Father-Tsar
  Narrates his fairy tales."

(December 20-24, 1818)

Alexander, in part, was brought up in the military, parade ground atmosphere favored by his martinet of a father, Paul I (1796-1801). Alexander played a leading role in the coalitions aimed against Napoleon before the two emperors made peace at Tilsit in 1807. At Austerlitz in December 1805, the French routed the Austrian and Russian armies after the Tsar decided on an aggressive attack. In 1812, when Napoleon invaded Russia, Alexander adopted the opposite strategy of retreat and caution, which some interpreted as cowardly. At any rate, after the Tsar's triumphal march into Paris in 1814, his influence on European affairs began to wane since his allies started to regard him as an impractical visionary who dreamed of a restored Christendom. A collegiate assessor was a low-ranking official in the Russian government.

---

## 12. ON ALEXANDER I

Our tsar was raised to the beat of a drum
And had a captain daring become:
At Austerlitz he had to flee,
In 1812, he proved weak-kneed,
But, then, he was the front's professor!
But fronts on heroes start to wear—
He's now a mere collegiate assessor
In the department of foreign affairs.

(1823-25)

Alexander Zernov (b. 1781) served as a member of the staff at Pushkin's boarding school, Tsarskoe Selo Lycée, from 1811 to 1813. He apparently had a lame leg, a crooked nose and became an object of ridicule among the students. Both Alexander I (of the Romanov dynasty) and Zernov shared the same patronymic.

---

## 13. TO TWO MEN NAMED ALEXANDER PAVLOVICH

Románov and Zernóv the daring,
　　You're both alike besides in name:
Zernóv! You've got a leg that's failing,
　　Románov's head acts quite the same.
But where will I find in myself enough brace
　　With wit to end this likeness?
One in the kitchen fell on his face,
　　At Austerlitz his Highness.

(1813)

Pushkin's inspiration for this verse came from seeing a bust of Alexander I, sculpted by the Dane, Bertel Torvaldsen (1768-1844). Because of his vacillations in foreign and domestic matters, the Tsar was awarded the sobriquets, "Hamlet on the Throne" or the "Enigmatic Tsar."

---

## 14. TO THE BUST OF A CONQUEROR

It's useless here to see an error:
The hand of art has sure engraved
In marble, lips that tell of laughter
But on the brow, in cold gleam, rage.
There's reason for this dual expression.
Such was he, this sovereign:
Was given he to contradiction,
In face and life, a harlequin.

(1828-29)

Once again, Pushkin mockingly referred to Alexander I's continuous trotting around Europe and finds it fitting that the Tsar died far from the capital, in a port city on the Sea of Azov.

---

15.

He spent his whole life on the road,
And ended it in Taganrog.

(1825)

General Alexis Arakcheev (1769-1834) became Alexander's most trusted advisor in the last years of his reign. He earned notoriety as a brutal martinet, both because of his despotic control over Russia's internal affairs and because of the cruel severity of a soldier's life in his newly formed "military colonies." These settlements combined army service with farming and family life but became known for inhuman regimentation. "Loyal not Fawning" was the motto on the crest of the Arakcheev family. "To a whore . . ." originates in an obscene soldiers' song.

---

### 16. ON ARAKCHEEV

Of all Russia, oppressor,
Of its governors, tormentor,
And in Council rooms he's mentor,
While to the Tsar—he's friend and brother.
Full of vengeance, full of hating,
Lacking wisdom, honor, feeling,
Who's he? *Loyal not Fawning,*
While *To a whore* . . . a dirt-cheap soldier.

(1817-20)

In the military colony at Chuguev, in 1819, there occurred an uprising against the inhumane conditions; eventually 160 men were sentenced to death. In the same year, a German university student, Karl Sand, using a dagger, assassinated the noted German dramatist, reactionary and Russian agent, Augustus von Kotzebue.

---

## 17. ON ARAKCHEEV

He's a corporal in the capital—in Chugúev he's a
Nero;
But, everywhere, the man deserves the thrust of
Sand's stiletto.

(1819)

Alexander Sturdza (1791-1854) was an official in the ministry of foreign affairs and in 1818, in preparation for the Aachen Congress, completed a report for Alexander I on internal affairs in the German-speaking states that had recently suffered political disturbances; the report was published in November. Sturdza blamed all problems on the German universities and accused them of being comprised of immoral students and demagogic professors who fostered liberalism and fomented political extremism and disorder. According to Pushkin—like the fourth-century (B.C.) Greek Herostrates who burned down the beautiful temple of Artemis only in order to make his name immortal— Sturdza's accomplishment in life was to suggest razing the world-renowned German temples of knowledge. Sand knifed down Kotzebue in protest, among other things, against planned restrictions on institutions of higher learning, measures supposedly inspired by Sturdza's memorandum.

---

## 18. ON STURDZA

A soldier crowned you serve as lackey,
Your lucky stars be thankful to:
You merit laurels like Herostrates
And death just like a Kotzebue.

*Variant*

A soldier crowned you serve as lackey,
But I don't give a fuck for you:
You merit laurels like Herostrates
And death just like a Kotzebue.

(1819)

The Bible Society was founded in London in 1804 and opened a branch in St. Petersburg in 1812. It had the praiseworthy philanthropic aim of translating Scripture into the vernacular and distributing easily affordable copies among all classes of society, with the poorest receiving them *gratis*. By 1822, the Russian Bible Society had printed 129 editions in twenty-nine languages and distributed 675,000 copies in the Empire. However, since Alexander I gave warm moral and financial support to the enterprise, the Society also became a center of power; in time, access to high office and the court depended on one's belonging. Consequently, the Society attracted opportunists as well as believers. For Pushkin, Sturdza symbolized the many hypocritical or cynical members who professed the Bible Society's religiosity only to remain close to the Tsar's inner circle.

---

## 19. ON STURDZA

I walk around Stúrdza,
Stúrdza the biblical;
I gaze upon Stúrdza,
Stúrdza monarchical.

(1819)

Some members of the Russian church hierarchy also obsequiously supported the Bible Society, despite its ecumenical, non-Orthodox tendencies.

---

20.


The Bible men enjoy such bliss,
Their asses boast such cleanliness;
The monks just lick their sirs—
The holy low-down curs!

(1819)

Count Alexis Razumovsky (1748-1822) was minister of education from 1810 to 1816 and therefore was responsible for Pushkin's Lycée. Razumovsky (whose name comes fromt he Russian root word for intellect) was well educated and dabbled in botanical research. However, he had little interest in his job and was, besides, reactionary in his political, social and educational views. The observant young Pushkin surmised that the Count wanted, above all, to receive the high order of St. Andrew First Class, whose bearers wore a light blue ribbon. Pushkin clearly thought the man did nothing to deserve the honor, and indeed he never got it. Furthermore, the poet seemed to think that Razumovsky had outlived his time on earth.

---

## 21. ON COUNT A. K. RAZUMOVSKY

Oh bless my soul, there's something
That I have heard amusing:
A ribbon blue they gave unto a man of learning.
—So let him be! There's no one I detest:
Please that God may also bless him with eternal rest.

(1814-16)

This epigram was directed against Prince Alexander Golitsyn (1773-1844), who was appointed minister of education and spiritual affairs in 1817. A fervent member of the Bible Society, Golitsyn preferred piety to secular knowledge and questioned the value of higher education. An intricate plot, led by Orthodox prelates who resented the foreign origins of the Bible Society, resulted in his "resignation" in 1824. One of the accusations against Golitsyn was his friendship with Alexandra Khvostova (1768-1853), who presided over a religious salon and wrote brochures on mysticism of the flagellant type. Another insinuation was that Golitsyn was involved in a homosexual relationship with V. N. Bantysh-Kamensky of the foreign affairs ministry.

---

## 22. ON PRINCE A. N. GOLITSYN

Here we have Khvostóva's protector,
Here we have the soul of a slave,
Education's chief destructor,
Protector of Bantýsh, the knave!
For God's sake, put pressure on him,
From all sides attack withal!
From behind shall we not try him?
That's his weakest side of all.

(1824)

The Princes Alexander (1788-1866) and Ivan (1789-1869) Lobanov-Rostovsky argued at a meeting of the State Council in 1824 in defense of retaining flogging as an instrument of punishment—except for pregnant woman and breastfeeding mothers.

---

23.

Oh princes, eminent patricians,
Who knout and lash do justify,
All of our women and our children
To you are grateful, as am I.
For you to God will I be praying
And never you I'll be forgetting.
When e'er . . . they embar
Me to get . . . my flogging,
To your great health and standing,
My first whip lash I'll give the tsar.

(1825)

Count Michael Vorontsov (1782-1856), as governor-general of New Russia, had charge of Pushkin when he lived and worked in Odessa in 1823-24 during his banishment from the capital. The two came to dislike each other intensely, each sought to humiliate the other, and finally Pushkin was forced to leave the city and spend his remaining years in exile at his mother's rural estate.

At first, Vorontsov tried to make Pushkin his court poet, a patronizing attitude the ever-proud artist could not abide. Pushkin satirized Vorontsov's inability to appreciate true art (especially Pushkin's of course) by comparing him to Midas, the mythological Greek king whose ears Apollo changed into those of an ass for preferring Pan's music to his. In general, Vorontsov's duplicitous character and pretensions irked Pushkin. The Count's anglophilism was picked as a special target: he was educated in England, spoke Russian with an English accent and liked surrounding himself with English servants and being called "milord." Also, in Pushkin's opinion, Vorontsov's interest in the commercial operations of the Odessan port bespoke affinity to the bourgeoisie, not the nobility.

Besides authoring the following three epigrams, which rapidly made the rounds in Odessa, Pushkin avenged himself by courting, not unsuccessfully, Vorontsov's wife, Elizabeth.

---

24.

'Though not midst us, but where I can't record,
The venerated Midas was milord.
He had a soul banal and lowly—
So not to fall on paths oft slippery,
To well-known rank he crawled with aim
And thus a well-known man became.
But one more word about this Midas:
He didn't possess among his assets
Ideas, plans that were profound:
His mind to mediocrity was bound.
His soul possessed but little valor;

But then, he was so pompous, strained and
                                         mannered.
My hero's many flatterers,
Not knowing how to praise their sir,
Decided to proclaim him crafty . . .

(1824-27)


## 25. ON VORONTSOV

Half milord, and half a tradesman,
Half a savant, one half a dunce,
Half a cad, but here's for once
A hope he'll yet become a full one.

(1824)


## 26. ON VORONTSOV

The singer David, small of stature,
Goliath nonetheless did rout,
Who was a general of much matter,
I'll swear, no lower than a count.

(1824)

Peter Chaadaev (1794-1856) was an army officer, writer and philosopher whose most famous work is the *Philosophical Letters,* a critique of Russia for which officials declared him insane in 1836 and placed him under house arrest. Pushkin met and admired Chaadaev for his progressive views on social and political questions while the poet was still a student at the Lycée. In Russia, being an officer in the light cavalry regiment of the Hussars implied masculine bravado rather than intelligence.

---

## 27. TO A PORTRAIT OF CHAADAEV

He's born by will of heaven,
Enchained to service of the Tsar;
In Rome, he'd been a Brutus, Pericles in Athens,
But here he's Officer-Hussar.

(1820)

Andrew Muravyov (1806-74), author of books on spiritual topics and an official in the ministry of foreign affairs, frequented, along with Pushkin, the salon of Zinaida Volkonskaya. At her home in 1827, Muravyov, also an aspiring but uninspired poet, clumsily knocked over a plaster statue of Apollo Belvedere. Python, in Greek mythology, was a huge serpent, killed at Delphi by Apollo.

---

28. *EPIGRAM*
   (From an Anthology)


Twangs the bow, the arrow quivers,
And vile Python curls up speared;
And your face with conquest glitters,
Oh, Apollo Belvedere!
Who has come to Python's aid now?
Who your likeness bombardiered?
You, the rival of Apollo,
Simple Simon Belvedere.

(1827)

Although Pushkin considered him somewhat talented, he disliked Muravyov personally. Muravyov held a number of civil service posts and was appointed court chamberlain (*Kamerger*) in 1836, one of the highest ranking titles in the Empire. Pushkin, it might be added, was only a gentleman of the chamber (*Kamerjunker*), a low-ranking title usually reserved for adolescent noblemen.

---

### 29. TO ANDREW MURAVYOV

To Europe's and to our amazement,
A Chamberlain's high golden key
Was hung on an ass of great depravement
Which all found open anyway.

(1836)

Count Egor Kankrin (1774-1845) served as minister of finance in Russia from 1822 to 1844; he was known for his fiscal conservatism. He tried to encourage the flow of silver and gold back to the treasury by making them legal tender for the payment of government debts. In this way, he hoped to stabilize the ruble and eliminate depreciated paper currency, a policy Pushkin apparently did not appreciate.

---

## 30. TO KANKRIN

Russia puts its trust in Kánkrin,
And brings to him its silver!
He, in thanks for assets Russian,
Shits on it with paper lucre.

(n.d.)

In this epigram, Pushkin referred to several contemporary problems. The Kingdom of Poland staged an unsuccessful rebellion against Russian steward-ship in 1830-31. At the same time, Franco-Russian ties of friendship were weakened when Louis-Philippe—according to legitimists a usurper—ascended the French throne after the 1830 revolution unseated the Bourbon Charles X. The Baltic German provinces were part of the Russian Empire, but their nobility were often rightfully assailed for using their high positions in administrative, diplomatic and military service to preserve their outdated, exclusive privileges.

---

31.

It's feign to trust a gambler's honor
Or find in Poles for Russia ardor.
To trust a friendship French is also feign
Or thinking Germans serve not counting gain.

(n.d.)

Prince Michael Dondunkov-Korsakov (1794-1869) was a pleasant person but a man of few intellectual credentials. Nonetheless, in the 1830s he became superintendent of the St. Petersburg Educational District, head of the capital's censorship committee and vice-president of the nation's most prestigious intellectual institution, the Academy of Sciences. The minister of education and president of the Academy, Sergei Uvarov (1786-1855), appointed him to all these posts since he could trust him to do his bidding and act as his watchdog; in addition, rumors circulated that the two were lovers. Dondunkov-Korsakov irked Pushkin because of his role in censorship. Also, it seemed ridiculous to the poet that Russia's most eminent center of learning should have a "blockhead," *dunduk* in Russian—here, an obvious play on the man's name—for its vice-president.

---

32.

When the Academy meets,
Prince Dundúk finds there a seat.
People say it isn't fitting
That Dundúk this honor gets.
Why then do we find him sitting?
Since he has wherewith to sit.

*Variant*

When the Academy meets,
Prince Dundúk finds there a seat.
People say it isn't fitting
That Dundúk this honor has.
Why then do we find him sitting?
Just because he's got an ass.

(1836)

*Portrait of E. N. Ushakova with Feet*
Moscow, 1829

# III

# LITERARY FIGURES AND THEMES

*Portrait of Shakhovskoi with Asses' Ears; Theatrical Figures*
*Caricature of the Romantics' Crimea*
Kishinev, 1821

## 33. THE STORY OF A VERSIFIER

He notes with normal 'tentive ear a
    Bleat;
With just one stroke he filthies up a
    Sheet;
It's read to all, and all the hearers
    Gnash;
Comes print—then into Lethe's waters,
    Splash!

(1817-18)

Michael Rybushkin (1792-1849) was born in Kazan and published a historical tragedy, "The Taking of Kazan," in the popular journal *The Son of the Fatherland*. Pushkin thought the play well done but, when it received unfavorable reviews, Rybushkin did not defend himself, a lack of action Pushkin found stupid, if not cowardly; even at sixteen, he was a literary warrior.

---

### 34. ON RYBUSHKIN

A hero in the olden days
Would bravely rout his foe and, after completing his
foray,
Would hang his sword of war upon his country's
arborred rack.
But playwright Breaker, having finished an ink
affray,
Simply hung back.

(1814)

This epigram is directed against the Symposium of the Lovers of Russian Letters whose members resisted innovation and foreign contamination of the Russian literary language; for instance, they recoiled at the use of the vernacular, gallicisms or new forms such as the ballad. The Symposium was founded by Admiral Alexander Shishkov (1754-1841), and two of its leading members included the playwright and poet Prince Alexander Shakhovskoi (1777-1846) and Prince Platon Shirinsky-Shikhmatov (1790-1853), who came to occupy various posts in the educational ministry. The group was at the peak of its influence in 1815, but rapidly became passé as the New Style, fostered by Karamzin, superseded the Old Style among the upcoming generation of litterateurs, with Pushkin their triumphant light.

---

*35.*


A sullen troika now sings off—
Shikhmátov, Shakhovskói, Shishkóv;
One knows this fearsome troika well enough—
Shikhmátov, Shakhovskói, and our Shishkóv.
But who's most stupid 'mong this bad polloi?
Shishkóv, Shikhmátov, Shakhovskói!

(1815)

In 1815, Shakhovskoi presented a new comedy, "Lipetsk Spa, or a Lesson to Coquettes," which satirized the proponents of the New Style. The Karamzinists were especially irritated that the play enjoyed great popularity. They took to their pens and playfully dubbed Shakhovskoi "the new Aristophanes." In this mocking spirit, Pushkin joined the fray with his own epigram.

---

### 36. EPIGRAM

'Ristophanes did promise us the kind of tragic
                               drama
Where would from *pity* all begin to wail,
Where viewers' tears would pour in rivery trails.
    Expected we a golden drama.
And then what? We sure got it, and well, well, I say,
One can't deny its worth and bearing.
Indeed, 'Ristophanes succeeded writing
    A truly *pitiful* play.

(1815)

Catherine Puchkova (1792-1867) was a writer close to the Symposium circle. In the newspaper, *The Russian Veteran*, she printed appeals for donations which were so sentimental and saccharine in style that they became objects of widespread amusement. In 1816, upon the death of Gabriel Derzhavin, the literary scion of the Symposium, she was criticized for not writing a memorial; Puchkova protested in verse that she was but a "bashful maiden."

---

## 37. ON PUCHKOVA

Puchkóva we really shouldn't gibe;
With pen in hand she does transcribe
The philanthropic views of weekly publications;
While veterans she helps, she offers readers
                                    joculation.

(1815)

## 38. ON PUCHKOVA

Oh why cry out that you're a *virgin*
In ev'ry virginal rondelle?
Oh, see I now, thou Eve of songdom,
A bridegroom's what you hope to fell.

(1816)

Theodore Glinka (1786-1880) was a poet, publicist and Guards officer. Associated with the Old Stylists of the Symposium, Glinka published transpositions of psalms in journals, employed spiritual or biblical themes in his poetry and used the old-fashioned letter, theta, as his signature. Kuteikin was a character in Fonvizin's comedy, "The Young Oaf," a seminarian whose speech was laced with Old Slavonic expressions. "Rune" and "omega," respectively, are plays on the Old Slavonic term for the first letter of Glinka's Christian name and the last letter of the old Russian alphabet.

---

### 39. ON TH. N. GLINKA

Our *Theta*, friend, Kutéikin garbed in epaulettes,
He mutters to us some long-winded psalms:
Oh poet, Theta, don't become a rune 'bout town!
Oh sexton, Theta, you're omega 'mong us poets!

(1825)

Karamzin published the first volumes of his *History of the Russian State* in 1816; they traversed the reigns of the tenth-century rulers, Igor and his widow Olga, the rich civilization of the city of Novgorod, the Mongolian yoke of the thirteenth and fourteenth centuries and reached to 1560, the middle of the reign of Ivan the Terrible (also called the Dread). When he died, Karamzin had completed twelve volumes of his study, but it ended at the beginning of the seventeenth century. Pushkin's epigram indicated that he thought the task of writing the entire history of Russia too Herculean for any one person and wondered whether Karamzin should not have been satisfied with his 1795 tale of Ilya Muromets, an epic warrior of ancient times.

---

## 40. EPIGRAM
### (On Karamzin)

"Now listen well: A tale I shall announce
About the ways of Igor, then his spouse,
Of Novgorod and then the Horde called Golden,
Perhaps about the Tsar who's called the Dread ..."
—But, granny, what a senseless thing you've set in
motion!
Just finish Ilya's tale for us instead.

(1816)

Although the great poet, Vasily Zhukovsky (1783-1852), exerted much influence on the young Pushkin, as the latter began to mature and develop his own themes and styles, he started breaking his artistic ties with his mentor. The epigram parodizes Zhukovsky's sentimental poem of 1818, "Perishability," and repeats the first two and one-half lines. Pushkin then substituted his own last line and a half; Zhukovsky's ended: "What if that happened even with our hut?"

---

41.


Oh, grandpa, listen, everytime it seems,
When glance I 'pon the Retler castle olden,
It comes to mind: And what if this is prose,
And also bad at that? . . .

(1818)

Wilhelm Küchelbecker (1797-1846) was a poet, teacher, literary critic and editor whose participation in the Decembrist Revolt of 1825 led to his exile to Siberia. With Pushkin, he was one of the first students to enroll in Tsarskoe Selo Lycée where the poor fellow rapidly became the butt of countless boyish jokes because of his awkwardness, homely appearance and distracted manner. Pushkin was very fond of Küchelbecker (Willy or Klit) but could not resist mocking his early efforts to write love poetry and cunning satire, which were as clumsy as he. Hercules, the Greek mythological hero, excelled in making love but was intellectually weak. Nicholas Boileau, the noted seventeenth-century French poet and satirist, was accidentally castrated in childhood and grew up a misogynist.

---

42.

Here's Willy—he's so full of love's fire,
He aims his cantos low;
Like Hercules does he write satire
And loves just like Boileau.

(1814-16)

43. EPIGRAM ON THE DEATH OF A POET

Our Klit, deceased, won't be in heaven;
Committed he some sins accurst.—
May God forget his doings craven,
The way the world forgot his verse.

(1817)

One night, Zhukovsky failed to appear at a soirée. He offered as his excuse the fact that Küchelbecker had come to visit him after dinner, and he ended up with a bad case of indigestion. After Pushkin's epigram, "to be küchelbeckered" became a common expression.

---

44.

At supper I did eat o'er much,
And Jacob locked the door, he was incautious—
I ended up, my friends, as such,
Both *küchelbéckered* and quite nauseous.

(1819)

At the Lycée, Küchelbecker wrote Russian poetry in Greek hexameter, a style introduced by Trediakovsky in the eighteenth century. Pushkin thought the meter clumsy and preferred the Alexandrine verse form of iambic hexameter that the French adopted for translating the poetry of the Ancients. To add to the parody, Greek hexameter should not be rhymed. When the epigram on Klit was written, the battle between proponents of each meter was at its height. A decade later, Nicholas Gnedich (1784-1833) settled the matter with his brilliant translation of the *Iliad* into Russian using the Greek hexameter. Pushkin, while admiring the effort, still balked at the form and parodized the one-eyed translator.

---

## 45. THE MISFORTUNE OF KLIT

Klit, Trediakóvsky's descendent, in hexameter writes little
    ditties,
Like a fire-breathing dragon, 'gainst iambs and trochees he
    sallies;
Klit does opine that this simple meter ruins everything else;
It befogs many verses' meanings and cools a poet's feeling
    heartfelt.
I will not dare to contradict him, let him the innocent slice;
Iambs the rhymester may have cooled, but he'll turn hexameter
    to ice.

(1813)

## 46. ON THE TRANSLATION OF THE ILIAD

Gnédich, a poet with only one eye, renders for us
                                      blind Homer,
Only therein, his translation 'sembles the original.

(1830)

As mentioned earlier, Pushkin and other proponents of the New Style in Russian literature considered Count Khvostov's poetry archaic, lackluster and heavy-handed. This epigram poked fun at Khvostov's translation of Racine's "Andromache," the fifth edition of which appeared in 1821. It included a portrait of the beautiful dramatic actress, Alexandra Kolosova (1802-80), who was also connected with the literary figures supporting the Old Style and who played the role of Hermione in Racine's tragedy.

---

### 47. ON THE TRAGEDY OF COUNT KHVOSTOV
Published with a Portrait of Kolosova

A sim'lar fate awaits the poet
As for the beauteous one sublime.
His verse distracts us from her portrait,
Her portrait distracts us from his lines.

(1821)

61

Pushkin wrote this extemporaneous epigram while in attendance at a soirée where Khvostov, after lengthy readings of his poetry, excused himself to go to the privy.

---

48.


Although sympathy won't help,
For Khvostóv, I'm sad none worse
That he can't hold inside himself
Either his urine or his verse.

The following two epigrams were directed against Nicholas Nadezhdin (1804-56), a publicist, university professor and literary critic. In 1828, Nadezhdin published some of his poetry in the journal, *The Messenger of Europe*. Pushkin judged it ponderous, unwieldy and tongue-tied, completely in the school of Khvostov, the "Hoary Hisser," who patronized Nadezhdin. Hence, Pushkin trumpets the advent of the old man's legitimate successor.

Probably much more to the point, Nadezhdin, in 1829, wrote a series of articles critical of Pushkin's poetry. In the second epigram, Pushkin reminds the reader that Nadezhdin began publishing poetry at the age of twenty-four, but he at fifteen; he leaves judgement to Phoebus Apollo, the god of light and arbiter of artistic creations. In addition, Nadezhdin had finished a course of study at a seminary; in Russia, the name seminarian was often synonymous with an unlearned fool or lackey.

---

## 49. EPIGRAM

Oh hoary Hisser, you've reigned with glory;
It's time, it's time! Renounce your crown:
Your foster child is young, abloom and healthy,
You, he'll succeed, our poet of renown!
Behold: He hears, the eminent conversor,
The whim of fate is now becoming known.
Approaches he, the young successor:
Our Hisser the Second ascends the throne!

(1829)

A hymn was offered Phoebus by an urchin.
"He's well-intentioned; brains he's lacking.
How old is he? Yes, there's the question."—
"Fifteen? That's all?"—"Give him a spanking."
A seminarian next came bringing
A copybook of lackey's discourse.
To Phoebus page one was read by Horace
Who bit his lip to keep from laughing.
The reading made Phoebus heavy, narcotic,
In anger, he quickly stopped it.
He next told the full-grown nitwit
To go and run the gauntlet.

(1829)

Pushkin here mocked the dismal and cheerless elegies that were the fashion of the day and whose form, in his opinion, struck only a boring monotone.

---

## 51. THE NIGHTINGALE AND THE CUCKOO

In forests, in the idle gloom of nighttime,
The many-sided bard of springtime
Will warble, whistle and resound;
The cuckoo, though, seems so dull-witted;
It's egotistic and long-winded;
Its cuckoo only does it sound,
And then its echo it replays.
To tears have we been cuckooed!
Oh, save us, Lord; one wants to run away
From the elegiac cuckoo!

(1825)

Prince Peter Shalikov (1768-1852) was best known as publisher of *The Ladies' Journal* and the *Moscow Gazette*. As a poet, his work was characterized by a sugary sentimentalism that Pushkin found banal, although he liked Shalikov as a person. Upon hearing of this actual anecdote, Pushkin and another poet, Eugene Baratynsky (1800-44), wrote the epigram.

---

## 52. AN EPIGRAM ON SHALIKOV

Prince Shalikov, our newsman rather doleful,
Once to his family read an elegy,
The poet's chamberboy held the stub of candle
But shaking was his hand to great degree.
Then all at once the boy began to cry and whimper.
"Now see, you silly girls, whom you can take as mentor!"
In ecstasy he shouted to his daughters.—
"Confide in me, oh dear sweet child of nature,
Oh, why your eyes in silver do they swim?"
"I really need the outhouse," said the boy to him.

(1827)

The Prince Sergei in question probably referred to Prince Sergei Golitsyn (1803-68), also called Firs, an amiable army officer who dabbled in poetry and music. Although a dilettante, he apparently took himself quite seriously. In contrast to both his lineage and his aspirations as a poet, Pakhom is a common peasant's name.

---

53.

How awful for our native land—Lishchínsky's done in!
Prince Sérgei lives on still—take comfort gentlemen.

(1828)

54. A GOOD FELLOW

You're right—our Firs is learned but intolerable,
A pedant haughty and equivocal—
With airs so grand on all opines,
On all he knows indeed a tidbit.
I love you, Pákhom, neighbor mine—
Thanks be to God, you're just a nitwit.

(1820s)

Boris Fedorov (1798-1875) was a writer, journalist and prolific publisher. In good humor, Pushkin teased him about the publication of the *Modern Child's Library* (1828-29); it featured boring, moralizing tales for the young.

---

55.

Oh, please, Fedórov, don't come to visit me;
Don't lull me off to sleep—or, then, don't wake me.

(1828)

# IV

# JOURNALISTS AND JOURNALISM

*Head of P. Ia. Chaadaev*
Mikhailovskoe, 1824

In this parody, Pushkin pricked those journalists and censors whom he considered servile or erring in judgment. Sergei Glinka (1775-1847), a poet, publisher and translator, from 1828 to 1830 was censor of the *Moscow Herald*; by allowing into print a lampoon on Pushkin, he lost his position since regulations forbade *ad hominem* attacks. Michael Kachenovsky (1775-1842), as intermittent publisher of *Messenger of Europe* from 1805 to 1830, waged an unending battle against Karamzinists and Pushkin in particular. Paul Svinin (1787-1839), a writer, historian and publisher of *Notes of the Fatherland* from 1818 to 1830, praised Pushkin's works but was perceived as pandering to sensationalism and popular taste. Valerian Olin (1788-1841), a writer and publisher, earned Pushkin's ire by criticizing the "Fountain of Bakhchisarai" and for a faulty interpretation of Byron's "Corsair." Simon Raich (1792-1855) was a poet and journalist not much esteemed by Pushkin; in his journal *Galatea*, in 1829, there appeared an unfavorable review of *Eugene Onegin*. The poet quite clearly relished literary combat.

---

## 56. A COLLECTION OF INSECTS

What tiny specimens!
There are some, it's true, smaller than pinheads.
—Krylov

The insects in my collection
Are open to friends for inspection;
Well, what a family diverse!
For them where didn't I search!
Ah, what an assortment I've dug!
Here's Glínka—that's a ladybug,
Here's Kachenóvsky—a spider evil,
And here's Svinín—a Russian beetle,
Here's Olín—a little black ant,
Here's Raïch—a tiny small gnat.
How many of them are assembled!
Neatly, under glass and enframed,
They're through and through impaled,
Sticking out in epigrams, side by side arranged.

(1829)

Throughout his literary life, Pushkin fought the censorship establishment, whose approval one could usually obtain only by possessing the agility of an eel. Eerily similar images were used in the 1970s by a Soviet official: "You, Party editors, out to be an iron sieve, through which the author must crawl to press."

---

57.

If foolishly you'd start a-writing,
Then likely you would squirm and worm
Right through our censorship restricting
The way you'll enter Heaven's realm.

(1820)

In this epigram, Pushkin singled out for attack Ivan Timkovsky (1768-1837), the chief censor in St. Petersburg from 1804 to 1821 and a man noted for his severity, moralizing and petty faultfinding; he approved the publication of seventeen of Pushkin's poems but forbade "Rusalka." Alexander Birukov (1772-1844) and Alexander Krasovsky (1780-1857) joined the St. Petersburg Censorship Committee in 1821, and each earned a terrifying reputation among men of letters for being even more narrow-minded and tendentious than Timkovsky.

---

58.


Timkóvsky ruled supreme—and all aloud did say,
You'd never find two similar asses in the world today.
Appeared then Bírukov, and after him Krasóvsky:
And truly, wisest of them all, was the late Timkóvsky.

(1824)

Throughout his life Pushkin railed at the low quality of Russian journalism, especially if any article in any publication failed to appreciate his works as products of genius. The *Northern Star*, a literary almanac published by the Decembrists Alexander Bestuzhev (1797-1837) and Conrad Ryleev (1795-1826) from 1823 to 1825, contained literary criticism that praised most of Pushkin's work but took issue with the lack of civic concerns in *Eugene Onegin*; in 1824 Bestuzhev also published two love poems by Pushkin without permission of the author. The poet took his revenge, as usual, in an epigram that he wrote after one issue of the *Northern Star* was lost in the St. Petersburg flood of November 1824; thanks to Bestuzhev, the journal was reprinted and distributed by March of the following year.

---

59.


In vain was Europe gasping;
No trouble, don't be grave!
Though Petersburg was flooding,
The *Northern Star* was saved!
Your ark, Bestúzhev, is on shore!
The heights Parnassus stay a-feast;
And in a blessed ark once more,
They rescued men and also beasts.

(1825)

Egor Aladin (1796-1860) was a writer and the publisher of the *Neva Almanac* (1825-33, 1846-48) and of the *St. Petersburg Gazette* from 1831. In 1825, without asking Pushkin, he announced the poet's participation in the *Almanac*; this rankled Pushkin and gave rise to this satire. The verse was published in the *Almanac* the next year; assuaged, the poet continued making contributions until 1829.

Nicholas Polevoi (1796-1846) was a historian, propounder of the Romantic school in literature and publisher of the *Moscow Telegrph* from 1825 until 1834 when the journal was closed by the government for propagating radical ideas. In 1826, after calling Polevoi's journal the best in Russia, Pushkin began to bemoan the "ignorance" of his articles on literary criticism. Ivan Velikopolsky (1797-1868) was an army officer and writer of satirical and dramatic works; in 1826, Pushkin was angry with him for not having paid off a gambling debt of 500 rubles. Dmitri Kniazhevich (1788-1844) was a journalist, ethnographer and public official; the poet's quarrel with him probably came from his editing of the literary supplements to the journals *Son of the Fatherland* and *Reader's Library*.

---

60.

## To N. N.

The *Neva Almanac* accept from me.
It has nice prose and poetry.
Here Pólevoi you'll find right off,
Velikopólsky and Khvostóv;
Kniazhévich, cousin far removed,
Adorned as well this little book;
But you won't find me there approved;
My poems slid to Lethe's brook.
What's earthly glory? ... smoke and ashes black.
To me, more precious is your heart! ...
It seems to me, though, just as hard
As getting into that almanac.

(1826)

Pushkin tirelessly, and somewhat tediously, attacked Kachenovsky in a stream of epigrams, but there was good reason for this vituperation. From his podia as publisher of the *Messenger of Europe* and as professor of Russian history and literature at Moscow University, Kachenovsky waged an uninterrupted war against Arzamas, the New Style, Karamzin, both as a literary man and a historian, and then against Pushkin's own poetry and prose. Pushkin often dubbed Kachenovsky the modern Zoil(us), in reference to the fourth-century Greek critic of Homer and Plato, whose name became synonymous with a carping, petty faultfinder.

Kachenovsky provoked the first epigram by writing an article critical of Karamzin, whom—despite Pushkin's reservations about the thesis of the *History*—the young poet considered Russia's Tacitus. The last line of the epigram duplicated the one written against Kachenovsky in 1806 by Ivan Dmitriev (1760-1837), a friend of Karamzin. The line, in turn, is a literal translation of one in Voltaire's satire on his own literary enemy, the Abbé de Fontaine. Voltaire's original rendition has an untranslatable wit since "worm" and "verse" are homonyms in French, *ver* and *vers*.

---

## 61. ON KACHENOVSKY

Oh critic crushed by an immortal hand,
You have not earned a new disgraceful brand!
Is there a need in your disgrace to make a changing?
Calm down—and satisfy yourself with this old verse,
*From out of the ass of De Fontaine a worm degrading!*

(1818)

The *Son of the Fatherland*, from 1825 to 1839, was published by Fadei Bulgarin (1789-1859), another enemy of Pushkin. To repeat, pages of newspapers or journals were often used as toilet paper.

---

62.

The *Messenger of Europe* and *Son of the Fatherland*—
Of use for the mind, but better for the ass end!

Since Pushkin considered it cowardly not to flail back against an unfavorable review of his work, he composed the next three epigrams in response to negative criticism in Kachenovsky's journal of "Ruslan and Liudmila." Kachenovsky was of Greek origin, hence the theme of the first verse. The original version of the second verse used the name Liudmilin.

---

### 63. ON KACHENOVSKY

Swineopoulos! Incorrigibly flinging curses,
While you've grown gray in dust, disdain
                                   and darkness.
Calm down, old pal! And why this journalistic brawl
And all the tedious dullness found in libeling?
*The humorist's malicious,* Stupidity says all smiling.
*The ignoramus' stupid,* Wisdom says and yawns.

(1820)

64.

"Although he's fairly good as poet,
Emile is quite a *hollow* man."
—"And you are *full* of what, you stylish wagwit?
Oh, of yourself: I understand;
You're full of rubbish, my dear man."

(1821)


65.

How is it you're not bored with scolding?
My settling with you's short to proffer:
Well then! I'm idle, I'm not working,
While you're a working idler.

(1820)

Ironically, given the tenor of these epigrams, a favorite attack of Pushkin on Kachenovsky was to accuse the critic of making *ad hominem* remarks in his articles rather than concentrating on issues of literary substance.

---

## 66. ON KACHENOVSKY

Untalented in his slandering,
He sniffs for sticks and gibes,
But earns his daily living
With monthly published lies.

(1821)


## 67.

He hunts out journalistic feuding;
This soporific carping Greek
Dissolves the opium of his ink
Saliva from a mad dog using.

(1824)

Besides the usual jab at Kachenovsky, Pushkin here also referred to the contemporary fascination with Romantic elegies.

---

68.


Attacked by female indisposition,
Our Russian literature is ill:
She's prostrate and hysterical
And babbles in hallucinations;
And Kachenóvsky, frigid shrill,
Besides, for her, exposed to chills,
*The flow of monthly publications.*


(1825)

## 69. *THERE'S LIFE IN THE OLD DOG YET!*

What! Lives on still that journalist, Old Dog?—
Very much alive! But just as dry and dreary,
Coarse and stupid, torn with envy;
Everything gets printed in his worthless rag,
Trash that's old and any news that's trashy.—
—Ugh! That journalist Old Dog's become a plague!
How might one snuff this taper that's so smelly?
How might one get my Old Dog just to die?
Give me advice.—Oh well . . .he's not worth the try.

(1825)

Vasily Trediakovsky (1703-69) was a leading theoretician of the "classical school" of Russian literature who attempted to transpose French classical standards into Russian works and build upon them an original literature. Pushkin greatly admired his pioneering efforts but thought his style outmoded in the nineteenth century. Trediakovsky's colleagues in heaven—Nicholas Popovsky (1730-60), Ivan Elagin (1725-94) and Nicholas Kurganov (ca. 1725-96)—were representative of the intellectual pantheon of eighteenth-century Russia. Kurganov's *Writer's Manual* was a popular journal that contained a compilation of rules of grammar as well as collections of proverbs, adages and national songs. Pushkin, of course, implied that Kachenovsky belonged among, and wished he would quickly join, the dead writers of the old school.

---

## 70. THE LITERARY NEWS

In 'Lysium, Vasíly Trediakóvsky
(A man sharp-witted, who great praise deserves)
A journal planned and set to work with verve.
To help him out did volunteer Popóvsky,
Elágin essays promised to reserve,
Kurgánov was to take in hand the criticism,
Again would shine his *Manual*'s witticism;
And it was said that soon they would embark;
God will it so, it's such a worthy work,
And only waits Vasíly Trediakóvsky
The speedy coming of old Kachenóvsky.

(1825)

In an unfavorable review of Pushkin's "Poltava" in *The Messenger of Europe*, reference was made to the poet's addiction for writing abusive epigrams against the journal. The point was that most were unpublished, did not directly name the journal, and simply circulated among the members of literary salons.

---

## 71. EPIGRAM

When I muddied the face of the critic
With my satire naming none,
I'll confess: Unto my summons vitriolic
I expected no response to come.
Should these rumors be believed?
Really so? He did reply?
For his faceslap to receive
Did my fool go up and sign?

(1829)

In this instance, Kachenovsky formally complained to the censorship board that an article attacking him was personal in nature, rather than literary, and hence against regulations. Pushkin was delighted when Kachenovsky's objection was overruled.

---

## 72. EPIGRAM

The journals had offended him so cruelly,
The critic Pákhom grieved about it deeply;
In writ, he charged the censor with blame;
The censor proved right, we got a laugh, the critic
                                                was shamed.
Some types attack, of course, are deemed improper;
One shouldn't write: *That so-and-so old codger,*
*A goat in glasses, seedy man of slander,*
*And evil, base:* All *that* concerns a person's honor.
But, for example, one may print
That a Parnassian Old Believer gent,
(*In his own works*), of nonsense is the preacher;
He's wonderfully boring, wonderfully flaccid,
He's turgid, even rather stupid;
This talk is not about a person, just about an author.

(1829)

Nicholas Nadezhdin (1804-56) was a prominent journalist, literary critic and editor of the *Moscow Telegraph* from 1831 to 1836. In 1829, he wrote a series of critiques of Pushkin's works, such as "Poltava" and *Eugene Onegin*, in *The Messenger of Europe*, Kachenovsky's journal. The poet responded with three epigrams. He made the point that Nadezhdin, who was educated in a seminary, typical of seminarians according to Pushkin, became nothing but a lackey of the older man. In epigrams 49 and 50, Pushkin also accused Nadezhdin of being Khvostov's sycophant.

---

### 73. ON NADEZHDIN

While hoping for my stance disdainful,
The hoary critic me abused;
And patience now worn to a standstill,
An epigram on him I loosed.
Now bitten by desire for glory,
Expecting now an answer too,
The journal's jester, cunning lackey,
Would also write abuse.—Oh no!
In front of church, just like a devil
Who can't of Mass himself afford:
You lackey, stay you at the portal,
While I will settle with milord.

(1829)

74.

Into a journal, no wit European,
And over which an oldster pines,
With prose that's worthy of a peon,
There stepped a novice asinine.

(1829)

This epigram, also an attack on Nadezhdin, recounts a story told by Pliny the Elder about the renowned fourth-century Greek artist, Apelles, whose work a cobbler attempted to criticize.

---

### 75. THE COBBLER
   (A Parable)


One day a cobbler scrutinized a picture
And pointed out an error in the footwear;
The artist right away did brush in the corrections.
The cobbler, arms akimbo, offered more
                                        suggestions:
"It seems to me the face is somewhat crooked . . .
And then the breast, is it not much too nude? . . ."
Apelles then with anger interrupted:
"Pass judgment, buddy, not above the boot!"

I have in mind a man of my acquaintance:
I know not in what subject he's experienced
Or might excel, although with words he seems acute.
Some devil brings him, though, to judge the
                                        universe:
Let him try passing judgment on the boots!

(1829)

Among students of literature, Fadei Bulgarin (1789-1859) possesses one of the worst reputations in the reign of Nicholas I (1825-55). Born into a patriotic Polish family, as a youth he fought both in the Russian army and then against Russia on the side of Napoleon. Later, he settled in St. Petersburg intent on making a literary career. During the Nicholaevan era, he achieved some repute as the author of mediocre short stories and novels and, ironically, imperial favor as an outspoken proponent of Russian patriotism. His greater success occurred in the area of journalism; his newspaper, the *Northern Bee,* and the journal, the *Reader's Library,* enjoyed the widest circulations in their day. They achieved popularity, however, by catering to the lowest common denominator in taste. Pushkin, and many others with him, looked down upon Bulgarin as a venal hack, possessed of a mercenary attitude toward literature and one who acted as a spy for censors and the secret police.

The first epigram underscored Bulgarin's personal vanity, which seemed only encouraged by his bloated, homely appearance, and reminded the reader that his wife, Elena, was an erstwhile prostitute. The next two verses alluded to Bulgarin's ethnic origins and compared him to François Vidocq (1775-1851), the chief of the French secret police. The surname Figliarin is added since it comes from the Russian word meaning poseur or clown.

---

## 76. ON BULGARIN

In caring for your beauty dear,
You sprinkle rouge for looks so ruddy,
You shave your moustache and your beard,
You pluck the hairs from off your body;
That care is given for your wife,
For her with love you're ever blazing . . .
Fadéi, my friend, so I believe!
For whom, though, tell, your ass you're shaving?

The historical novel in question is Bulgarin's *Dmitri the Pretender*, a third-rate work.

---

## 77. EPIGRAM

It's not so bad, Avdéi Fliugárin,
That you weren't born a Russian baron,
That you're a gypsy on Parnassus,
That you're to all Vidocq Figliárin:
What's bad is that your novel bores us.

(1830)

## 78.

That you're a Pole is no taboo;
Kosciúszko's one, Mickiéwicz too!
Perhaps you are of Tatar kin—
In that I also see no shame;
Or be a kike—that's no sad claim;
The trouble's being Vidocq Figliárin.

(1830)

Prince Gregory Potemkin (1739-91), a lifelong bachelor, was Catherine the Great's lover and advisor; he exerted a strong influence over domestic and foreign policy through much of her reign. Bulgarin and Pushkin exchanged barbs about their ancestry. The poet was inordinately proud of his six centuries of noble lineage. Bulgarin liked to point out that Pushkin's great-grandfather was a Negro slave, sold for a bottle of rum. Pushkin countered that he became a favorite of Peter the Great and was by origin an Abyssinian prince.

---

79.

When I shall find Madame Potémkin
On dark Prechisténka Avenue,
Then let posterity place Bulgárin
Alongside me for equal due.

(1829)

Alexander Smirdin (1795-1857) owned the most popular bookstore in the capital and was also a prominent editor and publisher. Osip Senkovsky (1800-58), although an Oriental scholar on the faculty at St. Petersburg University, was of the same ilk as Bulgarin and cooperated with him in his publishing enterprises. Vladimir Sollogub (1813-82), another talented epigrammatist, wrote this extemporaneous verse with Pushkin.

---

80.


If you walk into Smirdín's,
Nothing will you find therein,
Nothing will there be to buy,
Just Bulgárin there to tread on
Or Senkóvsky to bump by.

(1836)

# V

# INDIVIDUALS

*Drawing of F. I. Tolstoi*
Odessa, 1823

Although Pushkin's genius glowed early—he published his first poetry at the age of fifteen—he was also a typical schoolboy. In this epigram, he demonstrated what became a lifelong aversion for hypocrites. While there is no firm evidence whose portrait this is, an educated guess might award the dubious distinction to Baron Modest Korf (1800-76) since later in life, as a prominent civil servant, he was noted for his conniving and duplicity. Father Martyn was apparently the religious instructor at Tsarskoe Selo Lycée. Lieutenant Colonel Stephen Frolov (1765-ca. 1843) acted as the school's disciplinarian, while the kindly Egor Engelhardt (1775-1862) served as headmaster beginning in 1816.

---

## 81. A PORTRAIT

Here's our chubby lad, our monk,
Warrior, scribe and poet.
Always and on every front,
Caning does he merit:
A regular priest when with Martýn,
With Frólov he's the mathematician;
Our hero Engelhardt walks in—
Asudden, he's the sure tactician.

(1816-17)

Pushkin wrote these verses on the eve of final examinations before graduation from the Lycée in May 1817. Theodore Hauenschild (1780-1830) taught German literature and served as acting director of the school from 1814 to 1817; he was a most unpopular figure. Jacob Kartsov (1780-1836) taught physical and mathematical sciences, while Nicholas Koshansky (1781-1831), a minor poet, taught Russian literature, at least when he was sober; student mockery of his adherence to the Old Style probably did not help his drinking problem. Ermolai Eberhardt was a tutor. The missing line probably comes from an old soldiers' song and relates to whoring.

---

82.

Hauenschild and Engelhardt,
Kártsov and Koshánsky,
And dancemaster Eberhardt
And Eberhardt Kavkázsky,
Like retired soldiers singing,
They all drawl so sadly:
"Gentlemen . . . . . ing
Lord, oh Lord, have mercy!"

God, my God, oh, oh my God!
Oh my God, my Lord!
Our sixth year we're heading toward,
Testing's coming 'round.
Well? What certifying
Did they give with difficulty?
"Gentlemen . . . . . ing
Lord, oh Lord, have mercy!"

(1817)

## 83. AN INQUISITIVE PERSON

—What's new? "So help me, nothing's new at all."
—Hey, don't be sly: you surely must know something.
How shameful, from a friend your own to call,
As from a foe, you ever all keep hiding.
Perhaps you're angry: why, good buddy, pray?
Stop being stubborn: give me just one word . . .
"Oh, let me go! This only will I say—
And it's not news—I know that you're absurd."

(1813-17)

Rufin Dorokhov (1801-52) was a well-known dueler and rake with whom Pushkin spent some time in the Caucasus in 1829. An army officer (although reduced to the ranks because of his behavior), Dorokhov also drew cartoons and wrote verse. Emmanuel Saint-Priest (1806-28) was an officer in the Hussars and a social caricaturist. Yury Neledinsky-Meletsky (1752-1829) was a government official, poet and transposer of national songs.

---

84.


You've had luck with ninnies charming,
Cards, the service and with feasting;
You're St. Priest as a caricaturist,
You're Neledinsky as a versist.
You've been shot through in a duel,
You've been chopped up in a war—
While in fact you're hero still,
Scapegrace, though, you are fullscore.

(1829)

Ivan Velikopolsky (1797-1868) was an army officer and author of satirical verses and dramatic works. In 1826, he and Pushkin lambasted each other in letters and epigrams concerning a gambling debt he owed Pushkin. In 1828, Velikopolsky published a poem, "To Erast. A Satire on Gamblers," to which Pushkin responded with an ironical verse and thus ushered in a further exchange of epigrams. Beverly was the eponymous hero-gambler of an eighteenth-century French drama, while Horace, of course, referred to the Roman satirist.

---

85.

Oh Beverly-Horace, poet-gambler,
You used to gamble off your piles of legal tender,
Your silver, your ancestral legacy,
Your coachmen, and what's more, your equerry—
And happ'ly on some card or even on a mav'rick,
You'd have staked your notebook filled with poetry,
If only any poem of yours were worth a kopeck.

(1829)

Count Fedor Tolstoi (1782-1846) paraded through life as a charming rogue who endlessly dueled, cheated at cards and drank heavily. He went on the Krusenstern circumnavigation of the globe in 1803-6 and, for bad behavior, was dropped at the Aleutian Islands; from then on, he was nicknamed "the American." In the first days of Pushkin's exile, he learned that Tolstoi had spread the rumor that Pushkin had been flogged during his interview with Count Miloradovich; this represented an affront to Pushkin's noble status since noblemen were exempt from corporal punishment. The poet responded with an epigram. Later on, upon return from exile, Pushkin challenged Tolstoi to a duel, but friends effected a reconciliation.

---

### 86. EPIGRAM
(On Count F. I. Tolstoi)

In a life, quite gloomy, scandalous
Had he long since been immersed;
Long had ev'ry corner global
Found profane his ways perverse.
But his ways he gradually mended,
Making up for his disgrace,
Now, thank God, he's only tempted
Up his sleeve to keep an ace.

(1820)

Apparently, Tolstoi guessed that someone else had attacked him in another verse, "To Chaadaev," when in fact it was Pushkin.

---

87.

Your guesses—they are all in vain,
My poems you could ne'er divine.
I know a cardshark you remain,
But have you lost your taste for wine?

(1821)

88.

Departed author, spare and puny,
He wrote for money, drank from glory.

(1828)

General Alexis Orlov (1786-1861), who eventually became a high official in the Russian civil service, met young Pushkin just after the poet left the Lycée, and they frequented the theater together. Despite the wounding nature of the epigram, the two remained friends. Eudoxia Istomina (1799-1848), a well-known ballerina in St. Petersburg, in the 1820s danced leading roles in ballets based on Pushkin's works such as "Prisoner in the Caucasus" and "Ruslan and Liudmila."

---

## 89.   ON A. F. ORLOV

Orlóv, in bed with Istomína,
Did lie in naked desolation.
The unreliable general,
In action's heat won no distinction.
Not thinking she'd offend her darling,
Laísa brought a microscope near
And said: "Oh let me have a glimpsing
Of what you fucked me with, my dear."

Nicholas Sipiagin (1785-1828) fought in the War of 1812 and, in 1818, when he married, was a staff officer in the Guards.

---

## 90. ON THE MARRIAGE OF GENERAL N. M. SIPIAGIN

As marital attire, it is right
That heroes wear their laurels;
Alas, Sipiágin's are so slight,
His bald spot's even unappareled.

(1818)

Conrad Dembrovsky (1803-34) was a ballet dancer and also aspired to a literary career. He wrote an epigram that commented on Pushkin's "ugly physiognomy"; the following came in response.

---

### 91. ON K. DEMBROVSKY

When into a looking glass I peer,
I think I see there Aesop;
But stands Dembróvsky at the mirror,
And of a sudden pops an ass up.

(1819-20)

Dmitri Severin (1792-1865), once a member of Arzamas and an official in the ministry of foreign affairs, quarrelled with Pushkin when they met in Odessa in 1823. Severin referred to Pushkin as an African, and Pushkin could not resist recalling Severin's humble origins: his father earned his way to high rank and his mother was the illegitimate daughter of A. S. Stroganov and a servant.

---

## 92. A COMPLAINT

Your uncle is a cook, your grandpa is a tailor,
But you, oh you're a man in vogue—
Or that's what people say, all to your favor,
And no surprise—since you don't stand alone.
Since I descend from noble stock,
Alas, among my kin no member
Can make for me a voguish frock
Or cook for me for free my dinner.

(1823)

Ivan Lanov (born ca. 1755), an elderly official in the Southern Colonial Office in Kishinev, quarreled with Pushkin at their daily dinner with General Ivan Inzov and called the poet a milksop; Pushkin then called him a winesop, and Lanov challenged him to a duel. Inzov forced a reconciliation, but when Pushkin discovered that Lanov had tried to trap him into getting flogged when appearing to make arrangements for the duel, he wrote the following epigram. The physical description, by the way, fits.

---

### 93. ON LANOV

Rebuke and grumble, king of ninnies,
Oh, Lánov, friend, you need not worry,
My hand won't give your face a slap.
Your ugly mug, all smug and pompous,
Looks so much like old women's arses,
That it can only beg for pap.

(1822)

94.

Prince G.'s a type unknown to me.
I've seen not such a hybrid worthless;
Composed is he of both conceit and baseness,
But in him there's more baseness than conceit.
In battle, he's a coward; in taverns, he's roughshod;
In anterooms, a scoundrel; in drawing rooms, a clod.

(1820-21)

Eustafy Rudykovsky (1784-1851), a physician, taught at the St. Petersburg Medical-Surgical Academy. He accompanied the family of General Nicholas Raevsky when they traveled in the Caucasus and the Crimea in 1820. *En route,* in Ekaterinoslav, they found a fevered, helpless Pushkin and invited him to join their party. Within a week, with the doctor's help, the poet recovered from his illness. Pushkin implies that Rudykovsky had also begun to contemplate a literary career.

---

95.

If you forsake the pharmacy for some laurel wreathing;
You will not kill the sick, but you'll put to sleep the healthy.

(1820)

Captain Ivan Borozdna (1803-88), later a minor lyrical poet, in 1822 was stationed at Fort Tishno in Bessarabia. At that time, a military court punished him for engaging in sodomy.

---

96.


Punish him, oh saints above,
Captain Borozdná, that shunt,
Fallen has he out of love
With Our Lady of the Cunt.

(1822)

Elizabeth Ogareva (1786-1870) was the wife of a senator and a social acquaintance of Pushkin. In 1817, the seventy-year-old Metropolitan Ambrosius of Novgorod and St. Petersburg, apparently charmed, sent the young woman a gift of fruit grown in his private church gardens. Pushkin played on the fact that the Greek god of gardens, Priapus, also doubled as the god of fertility and male prowess; he was usually represented as a grotesquely ugly man with an enormous erect penis. Priapus was also worshipped by those in need of great good luck, something Pushkin probably thought Ambrosius needed to woo Ogareva.

---

97. *TO OGAREVA*
    To whom the Metropolitan sent some fruit
    from his garden


The Metropolitan, a show-off shameless,
His fruit his own to you did send;
He wanted, clearly, to convince us
That god he is of what he tends.

All things are poss'ble for you, Woman:
Old age you'll conquer with a smile,
You'll make the Bishop lose his reason,
You'll rouse in him a passion's rile.

And he, now met your glance bewitching,
Will soon his cross then bid adieu,
Hosannas tender he'll start singing
To beauty heavenly, only you.

(1817)

110

Photius (Peter Spassky, 1792-1838) was prior of Yurev monastery in Novgorod. In 1822, he was elevated to the ecclesiastical office of archimandrite in St. Petersburg, apparently only because of the patronage of Countess Anna Orlova-Chesmenskaya (1785-1848). Photius' general popularity with women in high society, quite naturally, gave rise to gossip.

---

## 98. ON PHOTIUS

Half a fanatic, half a gyp;
For him are weapons spiritual
A curse, a sword, a cross and whip.
Oh Lord, please send us, sinners mortal,
Much fewer of this brood—
These pastors, semi-holy, semi-good.

(1824)

## 99. TO COUNTESS ORLOVA-CHESMENSKAYA

One woman, pious on the whole,
To God devoted full her soul,
But gave her sinful flesh
To Archimandrite Phótius.

(1824)

## 100. A CONVERSATION BETWEEN PHOTIUS
AND COUNTESS ORLOVA

"Oh, harken, what I am averring:
I've a eunuch's body, the soul of a man."
—But what are you doing with me then?
"I'm body into soul transforming."

(1822-24)

It should be remembered that at Orthodox church ceremonies, the congregation stands throughout the entire service. In addition, it was widely believed that seminarians were taught to sit while urinating.

---

## 101. THE BISHOP

The Bishop, isn't he still to us a holy presence?
Where people stand, he sits.
He farts into his vestment, and then they give him
                                                incense.

Pushkin wrote this verse on Easter Sunday when in exile in Kishinev. He was apparently rebelling against being forced during Holy Week to fast and attend the season's multitude of religious services.

---

## 102. CHRIST HAS RISEN

Rebecca mine, the Christ has risen!
Today I'll follow laws divine,
Bequeathed to us by the God made human
Who perished for the world wide;
I kiss you thrice, my angel mine.
But on the morrow, once you're kissed,
I won't be shy and I'll enlist
In Moses' faith, that's yours, dear Jew—
And, furthermore, I'll hand to you
That thing that warrants best a telling
Of who's a Christian or a Jew.

(Easter Sunday, 1821)

Alexandra Kolosova (1802-80) was a St. Petersburg actress who, in 1819, attempted the role of Esther in the Racine tragedy. Before her, the part had belonged to Catherine Semenova, a tragedian whom Pushkin greatly admired. Kolosova's forte was playing lighter roles, and Pushkin ridiculed her lack of natural noble bearing and of physical qualities associated with aristocracy, such as small feet and delicate hands. It should be added that the poet had something of a fetish about women's feet, especially if they were tiny.

---

### 103. ON KOLOSOVA

Esther's to us all-enchanting:
Charming is her speech,
Regal purple marks her entering,
Ebon curls her shoulders greet,
Voice so tender, glance so loving,
Hands all powdered, bleachified,
Brows all painted, over-arching,
And a foot of mammoth size!

(1819)

Nimfodora Semenova (1786-1849) became acquainted with Pushkin through her sister, the tragedian, Catherine. Nimfodora was an opera singer but owed her popularity more to beauty than talent. Dmitry Barkov (1796-ca. 1855) was a theater critic and translator of librettos who gave Nimfodora good reviews; he also frequented intellectual circles and served as an officer in the military.

---

### *104. TO NIMFODORA SEMENOVA*

Seménova, I'd like to be your bedspread
Or be the dog that guards your bedstead
    Or be Lieutenant Bárkov of the Guards—
    Oh, he's your guard! Oh, the blackguard!

(1817-20)

105.

Has Clarise but little money,
You are rich—go marry her:
She'd be becoming when quite wealthy,
While horns on you would look quite fair.

(1822)

106.

Lisa's scared to fall in love.
Say there, isn't this deception?
Hold your guard—perhaps it'll prove
That this Diana, goddess modern,
Holds a secret tender passion,—
Searching shyly midst you all,
With her glances' modest fashion,
For someone who would help her fall.

(1824)

The epigram concerns Todor Krupensky (1787-1843) who served under General Inzov and was the brother of the vice-governor of Kishinev. Pushkin was a frequent visitor at the Krupensky family home while he was there in exile. Apparently, the woman in question was Maria Eikhfeldt (1798-1855); she and her husband Ivan were also Kishinev acquaintances of Pushkin.

---

*107.*

Tadaráshka loves you sure
    For your feet so tiny;
And they're saying he'll procure
    Some odd sort of droshky.
Not so easily comes it to us:
    This is really so incautious!
Oh! In droshkies far away
    You can go, they all do say.

(1821)

Although Pushkin's amorous interests were constant and farflung, this quatrain seems directed at Anna Kern (1800-79), by whose beauty he was smitten; she, however, regarded the poet with some indifference. Anna had a reputation for forming liaisons, but seemed to find little joy in them.

---

## 108. MADRIGAL

In nothing have you found some bliss,
With happiness, discordant,
Your beauty's inaccordant,
Your wit as well is all amiss.

(1817-25)

Aglaya Davydova (1787-1847), the wife of the Falstaffian general, Alexander (1773-1833), met Pushkin while he was in exile in Southern Russia. She was included in the poet's "Don Juan List" (1829) of his female loves, as was Anna Kern. Agalya was a ravishing French beauty and coquette, who dropped her admirers unceremoniously. The following two malicious epigrams indicate that she would not yield to Pushkin's advances, despite his adoration. Liquid mercury was used at the time as a cure for venereal disease.

---

### 109. EPIGRAM

While leaving honor to a fate so feckless,
Davýdova, the furies' living victim,
From early years had loved the other sex,
Then punishment from Mercury brings sudden
                                    burden.
The time for penance comes unto her soul:
She lies abed; one eye is slowly puffing up,
And suddenly it burst. So what, you slut?
"Thank God! All for the best: behold another hole!"

(1821)

## 110. ON A. A. DAVYDOVA

Agláya mine one man has had
For being uniformed and moustached black;
For wealth, another—understood;
For being French, another—that's a fact;
Kleon—for wit that left her trembling;
Damis—for tenderly to her singing;
Agláya, friend, now tell me true,
For what your husband has had you?

(1820-22)

This epigram represents Pushkin's translation of an eighteenth-century French verse ("J'ai depuis peu vu ta femme nouvelle"), which in turn transposed a sixteenth-century Latin epigram.

---

III. *EPIGRAM*
   (Variation on a French theme)


So captivated am I by your matron,
That if my lot had been to be willed three,
Whose semblance matched your wife's just
                                             perfectly,
To Satan then would two I give up free,
If only he'd accept the third one.

(1814)

Dr. Pangloss, one of the central characters in Voltaire's satire, *Candide,* suffered from syphilis and, according to the author, lost his nose as a result. While it is not known whom Pushkin is warning, the disease was altogether commonplace.

---

## 112. EPIGRAM

Get treatment—Pangloss' fate will you appoint,
A victim clear of beauty's trap—
Or, buddy, will your nose be out of joint,
When for your nose there'll be a gap.

(1821)

# A BIBLIOGRAPHICAL NOTE

I.

Pushkin's epigrams were drawn from the following sources:

A. S. *Pushkin bez tsenzury*. London, 1972.
*Epigrammy*. Illustrated by N. V. Kuz'min and with a commentary of 17 pages by T. G. Tsiavlovskii. Moscow, 1979.
*Izbrannye sochineniia*. 2 vols. Moscow, 1978.
*Pol'noe sobranie sochinenii*. 17 vols. Moscow, 1937-59.

Indispensable for the translator of Pushkin is:
*Slovar' iazyka Pushkina*. 4 vols. Moscow, 1956-61.

II.

The annotations of the epigrams were not footnoted for purposes of simplicity and easy reading and also because the great majority of the information came from the general knowledge the translator and annotator acquired in doing research on the historical monograph, *The Origins of Modern Russian Education: An Intellectual Biography of Count Sergei Uvarov, 1786-1855*. Northern Illinois University Press, 1984.

The notes in the *Epigrammy* and L. A. Chereisky's encylopedic *Pushkin i ego okruzhenie* (Leningrad, 1975) were especially useful in providing additional details.

Besides the works cited in the introduction, other volumes that were consulted for the annotations, included:

Annenkov, P. V. *Pushkin: Materialy dlia ego biografii*. St. Petersburg, 1873.
Blagoi, D. D. *Masterstvo Pushkina*. Moscow, 1955.
Gershenzon, M. O. *Mudrost' Pushkina*. Moscow, 1919.
Ivanov, V. N. *Aleksandr Pushkin i ego vremia*. Moscow, 1977.
Miakotin, V. A. *Pushkin*. Berlin, 1923.
Slonimskii, A. L. *Masterstvo Pushkina*. Moscow, 1963.
Tomashevskii, B. *Pushkin*. 2 vols. Moscow, 1956-61.
Tsiavlovskii, M. A. *Letopis' zhizni i tvorchjestva A. S. Pushkina*. Moscow, 1951.
Tynianov, I. N. *Pushkin i ego sovremenniki*. Moscow, 1969.

III.

The following list represents a highly select list of works available by or on Pushkin in English.

Bayley, John. *Pushkin: A Comparative Commentary*. Cambridge, Eng., 1971.

Lednicki, W. *Pushkin's Bronze Horseman: The Story of a Masterpiece*. Berkeley, 1955.

Magarshack, David. *Pushkin: A Biography*. New York, 1967.

Mirsky, D. S. *Pushkin*. New York, 1926, 1963.

Pushkin, A. S. *Collected Narrative and Lyrical Poetry*. Tr. W. Arndt. Ann Arbor, 1984.

_____. *Eugene Onegin*. Tr. W. Arndt. New York, 1963.

_____. *Eugene Onegin: A Novel in Verse*. Tr. and ed. V. Nabokov. 2 vols. Princeton, 1974.

_____. *The Letters of Alexander Pushkin*. Tr. and ed. Thomas Shaw. Madison, 1967.

_____. *Poems, Prose and Plays of Alexander Pushkin*. Ed. A. Yarmolinsky. New York, 1943.

_____. *Three Comic Poems*. Tr. and ed. W. E. Hawkins. Ann Arbor, 1977.

Simmons, E. J. *Pushkin*. New York, 1964.

Troyat, H. *Pushkin*. Tr. N. Amphoux. New York, 1970.

Vickery, Walter N. *Alexander Pushkin*. New York, 1970.